The G

BOOKS BY JOHN N. MORRIS

John N. Morris

The Glass Houses

ATHENEUM   NEW YORK

1980

Certain of these poems first appeared in print as follows:
THE GEORGIA REVIEW, *The Autobiography, My Children's Book*
THE NEW ENGLAND REVIEW, *The Right to Life, Yearbooks, The Will of
    the Children*
THE NEW YORKER, *In There, The Examined Life, Wintering Over,
    For Julia, in the Deep Water*
THE OHIO REVIEW, *Lost Things, The Blacksnake in My Tree*
POETRY, *Archaeology, Map Problems, The Hours You Keep, The End of
    The Rental, Man and Boy, Halloween, The Christmas Letter,
    All He Knows*

*I am grateful to the John Simon Guggenheim Memorial Foundation and to
Washington University for the year of leisure in which a number of the poems in
this book were written.* J.N.M.

FOR ELLEN MAURICE

a belated eightieth-birthday present

I

II

III

I

ARCHAEOLOGY

Almost nothing mysterious is
To be found. This attracts us.
Seldom will we break into
Some Pompeiian perfect room
Preserved to us by a catastrophe
Or in the conservative bog unearth
Fresh evidence of an ancient
Accomplished intention, a ferocious
Strangling or its punishment.

These things we photograph.
Though our very air
Will make them decay,
We may treasure them on paper.
But such things are rare.
What we chiefly discover is
Neglect—the lost or discarded,
Each layer a different people.
What remains of them is
A good deal of inadvertence—
The broken vessel, the imperfect firing.
What lasts is the failure of skill
In a botch of approximation.

As if this were what had attracted us,
We carry it home, this waste,
To gaze on in the great glass houses.
The evidence surrounds us,
It gleams from every case:
They valued what does not survive
Like us. Or it is hidden from us.
This is what attracted us.
It shines to us, this waste.

THE RIGHT TO LIFE

In the novels I shall never write
The characters wait
For me to allow them to happen.
They have been patient there
In that nowhere for years
As in their causes.
But now they are stirring.

They say, *Instar the sky.*
Give us our children.
They believe in their lives,
The paper wind, the ink houses.
Optimists, theologians,
They suppose they
Would be made to suffer
To some purpose. They argue
As from a design.

They believe in their lives.
Because they are mine
I cannot bear to tell them
How in my words
I would find them wanting,
How suddenly some morning
I would tear them to pieces
Because they are mine
According to their deserving.

YEARBOOKS

Old times! Old times!
How gay it seems
To revisit the past
As if it were college!

There you are
Virginal and tense
In this print
In your freshman beanie.

You have nothing to do but become
A member of everything,
Year by year moving in
From the edges of its pictures.

There you have never been
Fired or divorced.
The whiskey is not drunk
In its paper bottles.

Still, the future is in you—
The half-life measured in losses;
What you will have to remember
A radiation in the bone.

There is nothing to do but become.
Turn the pages back to the beginning.
In the book you do not own
You have disappeared from every picture.

THE AUTOBIOGRAPHY

This is what you have come to:
In one of the last years
To make a beginning.
Out of the genealogies
Auspicious names
Glitter in constellation.
You are born
When you were born
At the top of the paper.
And your parents are there
Still, because you are.
You are getting them down
Here in the opening pages
Where you understand them.
Here is your childhood, here
You are home again
For thousands of words
In the perpetual garden.

Once you have buried your dead
At the end of a chapter,
One world is over.
The rest will seem
All plain prose sailing.
You are accurate even
When you do not remember.
For this is a story
That you are writing,
The story you tell
Of what must have been,
Your choices obvious now
Because you made them.

Soon the successful
Years ahead
You will put behind you.
Then you will arrange
The parts, settle the capitulation.
Should some things
Disappear in the revision,
They have never happened.
For a moment now
It all seems
To end happily.
In there, you are surviving.
You are there, you
Are covering up the paper.
You are there, who say
You have written me. I am
As you have made me.
Though I am in your hand
I live without you.
This is what you have come to.

MAP PROBLEMS

All this folding,
Confusing precision!
At first it's all
Too allegorical for words.
It's 1 : 10,000, each hill
Bearing its elevation on its back.
At first that's the problem.

Well may you thank God
You are under the instruction
Of those for whom
All the conventional signs—
For railroads and water,
For Forest, Coniferous, Fenced—
And the arts of Backsight and Foresight
By which you must learn to resolve
Every Angle of Doubt
Into its Point of Certainty
Are to be understood
In an obvious sense.
Their only wish is
That at last you should see
Something real perfectly.
(There in the margin
Where the annual declination
Of Magnetic from Grid
And True North is known
In minutes and seconds,
Even the future is shown
In naked abstraction.)

And gradually even you may learn
To learn to follow these directions,
To tell with this assistance
An Aerial Ropeway, say,
From a Road Under Construction.
Then it is time for your examination.
They drive you in the dark for miles;
They drop you off their map.
Now you must make your own.
You must follow it back.
Now here is the problem:
It stretches for miles,
It runs away,
The actual, in its own dimensions.
It's literal. That is the problem.

If ever you cross the line
With your luck and skill
Back into their big picture,
Then you'll feel safer.
That's natural. You'll have it all
Down on their comfortable paper.
With what confident strides
You'll inch through that theory!
Still, when you arrive,
Though you are grateful
For their instruction,
At last you have seen
Something real perfectly.
You have signed the wildness.
A name is written
On every body of water.
Perhaps you will never show them
Your copy of where you have been.

THE HOURS YOU KEEP

The hours you keep
Alone awake in the darkness—
From the dark bowl,
The water troubled by traffic,
How the light glances,
Glances into the darkness!
Now to the blind wall,
Now to the door, the ceiling.
The mind, the mind dances.
What hand can still it?

FOR CERTAIN OF OUR POETS

Having decided, were you free—
Free to enjoy a last afternoon?
So it is, of some, reported.

If we have been almost there
We think we can understand—
A piece of impertinence, the last indecency!
Perhaps we imagine a certain gaiety.

Or, lifting a last hand
Full of your will,
Will you have said,
This is taking years.
There is time to live forever.

THE RETIRED LIFE

At your windows I watch
You dine in another time
In a certain state.
The two of you become one
Of the laconic cultures,
A people happy around their fire
Speaking that quiet language
The retired life.

Now almost no one invites you
Anywhere even at the last minute.
Though you do not look lonely here,
Surely you know vaguely
That you are missing something?
What are you waiting for?
It cannot be us.
In the theatres in the cities
You still remember,
As images we blaze without you,
An imitation life.

This camera recedes.
I return to my life.
A god is in your fire.
You are still warming there.
Perhaps this is the last minute,
That point of light.

THE END OF THE RENTAL

The cameras are out now
In the last hours. This is the day
They turn over the houses. It's dazzling.
Their children pose, poise there,
Blind at the bright edge of something.

Last night, over the last beach fire,
While the Perseids showered
They sang their childhood
In the kitchen with Dinah.
Today they turn over the houses.
The weather now
May be excellent for others.
Summer is in the box.
They will take it away.

"Next year! Next year!" they cry,
They wave to the week's neighbors.
The last swim's over.
A line draws, the next wave
Comes ashore, it tears
Like paper across the picture.

II

MAN AND BOY

"You send us the boy; we return you the man."
A MILITARY SCHOOL ADVERTISEMENT

You will know that boy on sight.
In the advertisement
The same familiar gray
Half-inch face
Always arises
Out of its bell-hop collar—
The type of the boy
You are to send them
For the man in return.

They have kept that boy
In print these fifty years
In the back of the *Times*
Magazine section and the *Geographic*.
His head turned a bit to the right
And up, he stares at something
Serious a long way off.
You are the man
Returning that gaze. Unwearying,
He goes on
Being about fifteen
Forever, knowing
He will never return.

CONCERNING THE CHILDREN

How we tire of their
Ceaseless needing!
Give me, they say, *give me*
Your kind attention.

And we give it. They
Are ours after all,
Our own kind.
We give them their attention

And their food and enough punishment.
They are draining us dry!
Soon we will not have
Enough punishment for them.

If only we could
Ignore them,
As if they were not ours!
Perhaps then they might

Go away like the neighbors,
Like other people's lives.
Give me my sleep, we say,
Give me back my sleep.

CARNIVAL

Half the county is adrift here
Past the end of town in the 1940s.
It is the carnival. This August night
We home on this acre of dust,
We moon among the booths and rides
On this backwoods Broadway
In this itinerant village of lights.

Some few of us are here
To be superior. Ready for college,
We amaze ourselves
At our taste for these pleasures.
Therefore I do not care that here
My popgun will never bring down
The pack of Luckies with a bill snapped to it.
The only game I win is the one
Nobody loses, the Fishpond—
My prize three inches of compacted dust
Shaped and painted like Popeye,
A Japanese china cheaper still than plastic.

Nothing real of ours is at risk
Save the derisory sums we spend as money.
But though we are only slumming,
Perhaps we have also come
Here to be terrified mildly.
Thus we permit the Snap-the-Whip
To throw our weight around;
For ten cents a minute
It tries to tear our heads off.
And at the Dodgems the rural very young
Practice how they will almost kill us
In their pickups when they get their license.

But even the high-diver,
Though he is more like it, cannot alarm us
Enough. Though he himself
Casts himself down, he is only falling
Skillfully, and scandal says
There's a trick to it, a false bottom.

But what is that sound
We have been hearing
Down at the end of the light
At the end of the midway where the pines
Begin again as dark as Germany?
Something is trying
To get out of something—
The motorcycle rider in his drum!
The best is last. It sounds
Like an iron lion roaring.

Up on the rim for our fifty cents
Forty or so of us jostle to stare down
Into the pit into what prepares for us.
Or does not prepare. He ignores us
In his boots and greasy jeans.
(Though his helmet looks as if it flew
The mails with Lindbergh, he will not descend
To costume; only his assistant
Or squaw does, garish in her tarnished spangles.)
Finger tattoos say D-E-A-T-H on the one hand,
T-E-X-A-S on the other.
He tinkers with the valves on his Indian.

It is deep in there, as if we looked under the ground.
Rough trade, he is the real danger
We have been looking for. He would as soon
Beat the shit out of each of us with a tire iron
As look at us. But tonight he will entertain us.
He is going to almost die before us, right in our faces.
He is going to drive that shiny ton
Up to us around what in the carnival
They call the Wall of Death—and now he's doing it!
Her mike says *Here . . . he . . . COMES!*
                                        Gyral,
Louder and louder he towers toward us.
Sidesaddle now in this wooden, slamming *circus minimus*,
His physics is doctoral: what holds him up

Flings him away. He's swung like milk in a bucket
That never spills a drop. Up on the rim we say
That boy can evermore ride that Indian!
He is trying to get out if it kills him
And a dozen of us. But now he gives up,
Shuts off in his circles at sixty
Three feet from our faces. In parabolas he winds down,
Falling away while the laws still uphold him.
On the ground he spits on the ground on our applause.
He will not condescend to face us.

And now we too turn away
From what he has done.
We shuffle down from our vantage,
Sheepish in our excitement—
As if it had been shameful in us,
Watching what we have been shown:
A man succeeding in failing
To die before us, in our very faces.

He was fighting to get out of something.
If he had gotten there, it would have killed him.
But he had to hurry. (If he had not
Done so, it would have killed him.) What held him up
Was his flinging away.
                              Now on the midway
They are unbuilding the booths and rides,
Taking to pieces those innocent delights.
The carnival is over. Under cover of darkness
They will all drive away
Into another county in the 1940s.
Now he will never get out
Of that hole in the air in my recollection.
Though he means nothing of this and I drive safely,
Beyond the evidence
I home on him these August nights
While the laws still uphold us
Whom they are flinging away.

THE WILL OF THE CHILDREN

He will not open his mouth
For the good doctor
Who must prize at it with a spoon.
He would keep his disease
To himself. He would die for it
If he could. Furious hands
Full of love must hold him down.

She will do one thing
Over and over, as at the piano.
Though she does not get it right,
She will not heed any instruction.
Though nothing is made,
Again and yet again
She rings out on the world like iron.

Even if it kills them, their will is
That it shall not be ours,
That it survive our affection.
How should we oppose it?
This is how they will become like us,
Their parents helpless before them.

THE BLACKSNAKE IN MY TREE

Somebody's bad idea
Of a pet, he is not seeking
The young birds
High in my tree.
He is looking
For something that feels
Like where he came from.
He is getting away.

Good sense says
He is the one afraid.
But how he glides
Over himself!
I cannot suffer it.
I hide in my house.
He is behind my eyes.
He is all things
I must not see.

This is the suburbs. I say
We are here
To put this nature behind us.
No one can own him
In a cage in the basement.
There is no keeping him
In, this bad idea.
He will get out. He ought to be
In the loft at home
Years ago where I do not fear him—
Invisible friend, best mouser,
Barn god, a rustle in the hay.
All evening I see him
As if I could see him.
I speak of nothing else.
He is mine. He is getting away.

THE KEY

What did we call it, the locked
Room at the end of the gallery?
Archaic, the business end a crenelation,
Bluebeard's key hangs by the roundheaded door.

I find in there
Hours of obsessed excitement
In the jumble and dust.
Among the scuffed transatlantic
Leather cases full of an empty sound
(Who arrives on the Mayflower, they say,
Returns on the Mauretania),
Oddments are discovered: one uncle's
Orange-and-black college mug
("The colors of Princeton," he says,
"The colors of Hell");
Mother's cowboy boots brought home from Reno
(Too large when I first tried them, then too small).
And the wooden basis of her second
Wedding cake. (On it, to please them,
I painted in the proper
Scarlet and gold a fouled anchor
Impaling the world—the Marine Corps emblem.
The eagle grips, surmounting all.)

Recollection sets hard.
Out of that stone I draw
Great-uncle Arch's gimcrack fraternal sword
Splendid as Arthur's
Under forty years of rust.
Over his head the true son raises
It, heraldic. I grip it, I claim him,
Father of my sons, going on before.

IN THERE

Into the rich
Last-century street
Where you are walking
Your night away,
A prodigal light falls
Over a railing
Out of a tall room
So private it closes
Nothing away.
You pause, you lean to it.
As if it could warm you,
It holds you here, this scene.

If you have everything, you have
Nothing to hide! In there,
Where it is all perfect,
As if she were waiting,
A woman is talking
To someone you cannot see.
And now she turns to the fire.
She holds her hands to the flame.
Suddenly, there is something
There you had forgotten.
As if theirs were your condition.
As if they knew your proper name.

If only you could
Enter there! If you could explain!
I am the lost prince, you would say.
I was born to this.
You would hold your hands
To their fire, the other life
Pouring out
Into the street
Where you are running now,
Where you are hiding,
Hiding in the dark, for shame.

LOST THINGS

Unimportant now,
But where are they,
The lost things—
Grandfather's studs,
The sword with my name on it,
My Best Student medal?
If to go warm were gorgeous. . . .
They are unnecessary
And that is why I need them.

Year after year
Things get away
From me, they disappear
From the bottom drawer
And the trunk in the attic,
Things one had expected
To be waiting at home.
I know they were here, I say;
They were here, because I saw them.

They are as real to me now
As the noise of the children.
I miss them more than the dead.
They were all made
Out of something lasting.
They are what I would keep
Until I leave them.
All night a light burns
In an attic elsewhere.
I am hurrying home.

HALLOWEEN

This is the day the children
Dress as the dead.
In their disguises
All evening they play
Hell with our evening,
Our terrors in their muslins.
Skeletons in high hats,
Perennial little queens,
They come back shrieking.

We are the kindly ones
And we feed them
Their annual meal, a handful
Of sugar the shape of corn,
Apples, a rope of black candy.
All year they starve for this food
In a trunk in the basement.
And then they are gone.
They scream back to their houses.

One day we will lay them away
Forever, the thin disguises,
Papery, perishing stuffs. They say,
The apples were full of knives.
We will never return.

THE WAY WE LIVE NOW

The way we live now
Is coming down the stairs.
It is saying,
"In the suburbs, there you feel free."

This is the morning.
The way we live now
Is shaven, is dressed
In the hair and hide of others.
Its house is paid for.
Its pants are pressed.

Now the way we live now
Is driving to work
That commands respect.
At last it is like the others
Who are happier than the rest.

KEEPING US WARM

1. *The Heating Bill*

It rises like what it is charging for.
As if the whole house were a chimney,
I send up a column of heat
In sacrifice to heaven. Each month I pay
My demon in the basement, that consuming spirit,
A week of my work. Whole days go up in smoke.
I appease my *lares* and *penates* with therms.

And though I have at my hearth a cunning device
For making logs by rolling up my old dollars,
The cold still finds us.
At every window and cranny
The whole winter is coming in
Out of the street to get warm
And there is no stopping it.
Though the president suggests
I stuff each orifice with my tax money,
I do not have enough.
On each sill the copper stripping sings
Like the reed of an Aeolian woodwind.
There is nothing to do. Turn the thermostat up
Until we are all absolutely roasting!

2. *Family Dinner*

But what are we cooking here
At this great expense
In this eight-room oven?
And for whose tasting?

Though it is roasting in here (the preferred
Method for the best cuts), modesty says
This is only a stew we have gotten ourselves into.
But even a meat-and-potatoes cuisine
Is the art of controlled decay and we
Are breaking down rapidly in an orderly fashion.
By the action of our heat the connective tissues
And the serum of the blood reduce to a sapid jelly,
And the coarsest and toughest parts, the odd pieces
Of meat and trimmings, the orts and bones
Become tender and digestible. This is delicious!
The consuming fire brilliant in our faces,
We make this rich meal for us every evening.
In the morning we come down ravenously hungry.
We are pale as the breath that plumes before us.
Because we cannot afford not to,
We turn up the generous heat once again.

THE MEXICAN BOWL

were I any good
with my hands
with my hands
I would make again
the Mexican bowl
we bought for our wedding
complete with the invisible
thread through it
at last it could only
break in our hands
in our hands only

MY CHILDREN'S BOOK

This story goes on a long time,
Children, and how shall I appear
For years in your translations?
As the kind bear I am
In our polite family mythology?
Or Mr. Fear-in-the-Forest, the Man
Who Made the Mountains?

                  No.
All Sunday in your recollection
I grouse in my chair in our story
Reading my dull thriller,
The Case of the Ordinary Man,
Quickly through to the predicted end.

And do not wish to be interrupted.
Not much is true, we know, in our story.
Still, in it each of us gets something
He wishes. And what that comes to.
We are writing it now. You
Are taking it down
In part from my dictation. This
Is one book I shall not finish. I
Leave it to you. I
Wish I could see how it will end, I
Wish you could tell me. This
Is the exciting part, do not interrupt me.

LOCAL KNOWLEDGE

Prospect Hill, Oneida County, New York

It takes local knowledge
To know its name
Is worth the visit.
The afternoons we drive
A dull spirit to it, I say
We come here to have it
Disappoint us, be somewhere
Else to turn our backs on.
I say we arrive to leave.
But still we stay.

We've come for the elevation.
Between clouds that hurry to be
New England's weather,
Over the October fields
Acres of illumination
Hasten toward us.
We have come to be
The center of something,
The round world
Falling away.
We stay for the distance—
These miles of Upstate
American absence
Tutorial and gay.

THE CHRISTMAS LETTER

Wherever you are when you receive this letter
I write to say we are still ourselves
In the same place
And hope you are the same.

The dead have died as you know
And will never get better,
And the children are boys and girls
Of their several ages and names.

So in closing I send you our love
And hope to hear from you soon.
There is never a time
Like the present. It lasts forever
Wherever you are. As ever I remain.

III

THE EXAMINED LIFE

"Were it possible for us to wait for ourselves to come into the room, not many of us would find our hearts breaking into flower as we heard the door handle turn."

REBECCA WEST, *A Train of Powder*

Surely there are certain of you
You have left behind you
Whom you would welcome?
But which are they?
Where is the boy who looked after the sheep?
He is under the haycock. He has gone
Where they go after you count them.

Even so, none of you would ever come
Pert and whistling to that door
Like the mailman careless of the terrible
Letter he leaves you, the news
That shakes in your hand on the rattling paper.

No. You will come to you
Like the doctor
Heavy with what he has to tell you.
His hand turns the slow doorknob.
He cannot bear what he faces.

WHAT THE RATCATCHER SAID

Gray or brown, he contends
Invisibly for our houses.
You will never see him alive.
For you he is his effects.
You fear for the children.

Therefore I leave for him
For you favorite poisons
Unspeakable in their operation.
Even to these he adapts.
He contemns our oblations.

Though I am beside you
The war is in the blood.
The two species agree
In their predaceous habits,
Omnivorous diet and great fecundity.

The incisors grow
Continually and must be
Worn off equally fast.
In both kinds,
He is grinding them down
In the dark in the foundation.

THE NEEDIEST

They are undesirable now.
No one could want them
In their one-room,
Lonely, unheated, trite
Apartments we read of
At Christmastime in the papers.

Only there dare we behold them—
Or asleep in a doorway at Macy's.
They rustle like mice in a wastebasket,
Their clothes stuffed
Full of the *Times* to keep them warm.

We say they are the neediest cases.
They do not enjoy their lives
And we are the last to blame them.
Though no one supposes
They are like us at all now,
They know what we are learning
While we are reading the papers.
They know what they are worth.
They know they are undeserving.

FOR JACK MEEKE, A.M. (OXON.)

"We then called on the Reverend Mr. Meeke, one of the fellows, and of Johnson's standing. Here was a most cordial greeting on both sides. On leaving him, Johnson said, 'I used to think Meeke had excellent parts, when we were boys together at the College. . . . I remember, at the classical lecture in the Hall, I could not bear Meeke's superiority, and I tried to sit as far from him as I could. . . . About the same time in life, Meeke was left behind at Oxford to feed on a Fellowship, and I went to London to get my living: now, Sir, see the difference of our literary characters!' "

THE LIFE OF JOHNSON

They could not bear our superiority and we
Could not forsake it. Jack, they despise us!
Yet there is something here
They seek. They come back
Out of their real world or Wall Street
To prove we are still here
To prove they were always right.

If they are rich or otherwise
Distinguished, the greeting is cordial
On both sides. We march them
In our procession, we doctor
Them up. And they seem to value
The leather medals we award them
For not being us in the hope
Of a few of their wooden nickels in return.
But the blessing they really desire
Of us we will never accord them.

Though we groaned in Hell, Jack,
In our padded Hell, we'd never tell them
We can scarcely contain our envy.
That is what they desire of us.
Jack, they fear us still.
That is why we despise them.

THE SURGEON GENERAL'S WARNING

Oh, throw the angry money away
As you step over the doorsill!
It is as worthless as love here
Which can cure nothing.
Though the bill is immense
And you cannot pay it
Even with your suffering
(Though that will be exacted),
This is not a punishment for anything,
But a result—something you have chosen
Forty times a day. This hell is just
A way of making you stop smoking.

Because you have refused to heed my warning,
You are as one of the children here
And must go to bed without any supper
For fear you should soil yourself under our ministrations.
In the morning we are going to take you away
From you for a really thorough cleaning.
(We decide and make the excision.
It is the occasion of our skill.
Which grows.) The interior life!
You know now it is not to be trusted.
This will teach you to take up smoking
Thirty years ago! Why are your hands shaking?
You are here to be made pure
Of the habit of a lifetime:
Pleasure we all know will die of itself,
But we are going to keep on killing
You until you learn
You have to live without consolation.

NIGHTCAP

Not for him the lucid, terminal martini.
Whiskey inspires the glass in this hand
To these swooping, tongue-tied gestures
At the ineffable or what need not be said
To be understood between us (though it *will* be said).

I am not drinking with this friend
And seem to have been doing so for hours.
Now at the bottom of the talkative bottle
We get down to what really interests him,
Which, as he says, is what he has always said.

He is not drinking with his friend
Either and has not done so for a year.
He is drinking with the amicable whiskey
And the tremendous sense
It suddenly is making in his head

Where nothing is a problem any longer
For the hundredth time for a few more minutes.
Now he blunders among a numb furniture;
Helpless, I help him toward the inconsolable morning
That waits for him in his insensible bed. .

CLOSING JACK'S

In dark Jack's on Greenwich
School's out now in our boyish, baccalaureate twenties.
A gaggle of college nicknames jams this bar
We think we have discovered—
Five booths and twelve stools
And a no-nonsense, pressed-tin decor.
We're in love with the authentic. It says
We're in New York and poor
Temporarily, our good education
Behind us, where we put it.

At ten on weeknights the industrious
Start to go home to their jobs in the morning
And soon our couple of scholars
Pursue their studies by subway uptown.
Twelve is pumpkin-time, says some wit
(He of the *tee martoonis*, and bad cess to him!),
When even our resident PR gal—
A tough nut in her heels and basic black,
Her latest coup a plant in *Women's Wear Daily*—
Beats it for her basement on Charles Street.
And now we have the whole playpen to ourselves,
We the hilarious, late-rising underemployed.

We are waiting here for us
To happen when we get older.
But only a few of us are going to make it
Until closing time, until our thirties.
(Down at the end of the bar is one
Who has the resolution
Required. Something has gotten into the will there
As if it were the woodwork. In the mirror
His mouth is moving. He is trying
To remember himself already.)
The rest of us will fall away,
The regulars who set out here
To sit out their twenties.

43

One by one they say good night
As if you would see them tomorrow
And disappear into some marriage.
Or their success overtakes them.
Soon you cannot remember
When you saw them last.

And now it is time that we too were going.
Leave him there at the end of the bar, that one,
His face in the mirror.
Finish the beer dry as a cigarette.
At the register a little late mathematics is doing
Under Jack's hair. He is counting our money.
Hurry! We are in
The corner of his eye. The rivers of Hell run through it.
All over town the last doors are closing.
Search your pockets for a single token.
From here even the end of the line
Is not far enough away.

THE ELIMINATIONS

At the beginning of the new age,
The age of the annual physical,
Of the prostate and the barium enema,
The serpent finger first explores the rectum.
The news is good for years,
You will be happy to learn.
As a patient you are a perfect failure.

But something inside you is entertaining
A sure and certain hope. You enlarge
Your repertoire of symptoms. You refine,
You rehearse them for the next audition.
You know you have to produce a sensation—
Something to make the doctor
Pick you almost alone
Out of the dull thousands.

Though any year the odds are long
Against you, in the end you will fail
To fail the examination. You will be successful.
Your reward awaits you. The knife is shining.
In the pure theatre you lift your eyes
To our eyes, the circle of your admirers.
We lean to you. I raise my rubber hands.

THE INFANTRY SCHOOL

Buck-naked you enter a new world
Coughing for the doctor. We dress
You for this life in a stiff sort of clothes
And begin the course of your instruction.

Though that starts with our way of walking
(A dull, practical kind of dancing by which we arrive
Everywhere together in time),
Chiefly we are a people of the book here.
In my hand I hold the manual.
In it we have our word
For everything. You will live by this
Like us, each according to his own copy.
There you will begin to learn
The General Orders and the care
And cleaning of your equipment.
Soon you will have your rifle
By heart. Though the manual warns
"This weapon shall not be assembled
Or dissassembled against time,"
Even in the dark you can strip it down
To its innocent parts rapidly.
On the firing line you acquire the whole art
Of action at a distance. "One click
Of elevation moves the strike of the bullet
One inch for every hundred yards of range."
You compose the sight-picture
According to the directions.
A finger tightens.
You release a little breath.

But though you have our word for everything,
It is dangerous here. And we desire your health.
Because you hurt in the School
Where you are alone by the thousands,
We show you moving pictures
Of the diseases of passion.

Though we teach you to disappear
In your clothes into the landscape
(It draws you in, it holds you like a breath),
We fear for the lives
That you are leading. So many things
You touch are poisonous or explosive. (In places
Even the earth retorts to the lightest pressure.)
That is why we keep screaming
Instruction at you:
How to shit in the woods
Cleanly, without any paper;
And the Three Rules—Stop the Bleeding,
Prevent Shock, Protect the Wound.

In the end, in the book of our words
Is no comfort. Still, in the years to come
You may remember all this fondly.
It was a little like a life, you will say.
You know the analogy is imperfect.
The General Orders do not apply
Any longer, and you cannot keep
Your equipment perfectly clean.
Still, the strike of the bullet is moving.
For a time to come
You will stop the bleeding. You protect the wound.
Like us you do not disassemble
Any weapon you have against time.

WINTERING OVER

The mail irregular
At best and the reception
Terrible always,
Day by day
Down the line
We let the electric
World in
A few words at a time.

Day by day we find
We have less to say.
In time we tune
Out entirely,
We hang up.
"This station closing down,"
I think we say.

But tonight is turning
The house against the storm.
In this bad weather
Where we are here to stay,
Stick by stick we burn
The last-century furniture.
Snow steers at the glass.
While we are warm
Not all of it
Will get away.

ALL HE KNOWS

My dog knows the garbagemen,
Those ruffians out in the alley
In their noisy, enormous truck,
And what they are up to:
They are stealing our garbage.
He's furious about it.
This has got to stop, he seems to say.
Twice a week they come and just
Take it away and you do nothing.
Yes. He makes sense in his way,
The way sense does. He does not know
Where it is going, some deep hole
Into the west county, gehenna, a place
Of permanent burning. All he knows
Is what he sees, how all day she
And I carefully feed into the special box
In the special corner all manner
Of deliciousness, spilling nothing; then
In a procession of one as if it were precious
She or I every day
Carry it out to the great
Cans where we store it—
Our effects, the proof of the pudding, the eating.
All he knows is,
Everything ends up there. And gets taken away.

ON THE STAIRS

The knife in the black hand is at her throat.
But these are her stairs they are standing on
Where nothing bad can happen in our forties;
And so this cannot be true. Yet the knife hand is steady.

Sex is a little on his mind—as a convention, a duty
To the occasion. He gropes her without conviction.
He really desires money and she does not have enough.
She would not have enough if she had a million
To make him back out into the moment before the morning
Stopped being dull forever. So they are at a standstill.

They are at a standstill. They are caught up
In the tense trance of something about to happen,
No one knows what. How shall they be delivered?
The knife's touch perhaps shall bring them both to life?
(In fact, a bell will, an innocent suburban
Errand at the door. It will cut them
Apart, it will dissolve their courage, free them
To fly from one another. But we cannot tell
Yet that this is how it will turn out.)
They stand still and they stare at the knife hand
As if perhaps *it* knew what is going to happen.

I witness to this: though it is only a story
I am telling, I cannot make it end
Fairly happily (though it does: there! the bell rings
To release them) as I cannot keep it from having happened
Forever. Still, on these stairs of mine in my story
That I am telling you to entertain you
She is still standing still and we are
Holding our breath, holding the knife hand steady.
We are going to keep on doing this until I release you.

AT THE DEATH OF GULLIVER

How you discovered me here
In my little garden at Redriff
I am incurious to know
And can tell you nothing
That you would like to learn.
Which was the worst
Of all my voyages?
But I have told you
Without equivocation
Or the lie of metaphor
And have listened for years
To you reading me perfectly
Without comprehension.
Now I cannot remember
In our new speech
That thinks perfection
Is dull, is death,
What I thought in a book
In a style I have forgotten.

But certainly it was not
My trip to the small
With their compassable malice
Nor yet to the unchristian
Horses we no longer understand.
It was none of these, it is . . .
(*Aposiopesis!* Do you know the term?)
The sun shines weakly here
On my age in my garden.
These afternoons I think of Glumdalclitch,
My little nurse. Is she dying now
Her enormous death?
                                Look!
The great birds! There!
The great birds of that country!
The huge dead are ever among us.
They stand about us in their thousands.
I think only of a vast kindness.

THE COMMON LIFE

He walks the dog and enjoys it,
She does the dishes and doesn't.
It's the usual story: a good marriage.
This is the Honor Farm, the open prison
They are trapped in voluntarily.
In the bank his retirement grows
Larger and nearer. When the dog dies
They will begin to travel widely.
Now they take turns taking out the garbage.

And do not stray from the reservation
They have made of themselves, a joint resolution.
Though how they came here to the everyday
That they are so patient in
Is a story as dull to us as wedding pictures,
To them it comes back like re-runs
Of an early work of one of the classic directors.
Does it matter, then, that nobody much likes them—
Her exhausting charm, his suburban opinions?
This does not occur to them.
They have their children to worry about
And the plans for next summer:
The daughter who marries
Early and often, the son who never does;
The ocean or the mountains.
To themselves they are only themselves.
Till ten she yawns in her chair;
He stares into the deep whiskey.

And almost nothing ever happens.
We say, *What is the matter with them?*
They ought to be dying of boredom.
But they know they are not in
All this simply for the fun of it.
If they are the open book we say,
It is a work of some distinction,
A life. Though it seems to go on

Forever, it will not really take long
To finish it—and things
Almost always liven up at the end.

If we do not understand this
Because we are not like them
Something important has escaped us.
I do not mean love, our favorite possession.
But something. Whatever it is,
In the end, in the surgical Hilton
Where we go to die in misery in comfort,
They will hold on like grim
Death to it. This is the Honor Farm.
Though it may bore us, bore us to extinction
Because we are not like them
We fear something is making them terribly happy.

AT KILROY'S GRAVE

Kilroy is here. Under one of his names
This descendant of a long line
Of initials incised in the skin of trees—
Impertinent, especially active in time
Of war and cheerful in the cause—
At last resigns the strenuous commission.

Though, contrary to popular report,
This restlessness no one has ever seen
Had other messages ("Wash me,"
His finger might say on the dusty car,
Indignant on behalf of the mechanical),
It is true that above all things
Places he loved. Latrine
By latrine he civilized the ground.
Even at the Hot Gates his alert pencil
Went before us. We found this calming.

He made a place for us everywhere,
Signing it. *Here* became where he had been.
We know what his stone says without reading it.
Wherever we go he precedes us.
Kilroy, we greet you. Here we say what you say:
I came, I saw. Hail and farewell.
We who are about to move on salute you.

FOR JULIA, IN THE DEEP WATER

The instructor we hire
Because she does not love you
Leads you into deep water,
The deep end
Where the water is darker.
Her open, encouraging arms
That never get nearer
Are merciless for your sake.

You will dream this water always
Where nothing draws nearer.
Wasting your valuable breath
You will scream for your mother—
Only your mother is drowning
Forever in the thin air
Down at the deep end.
She is doing nothing,
She never did anything harder.
And I am beside her.

I am beside her
In this imagination.
We are waiting
Where the water is darker.
You are over your head.
Screaming, you are learning
Your way toward us,
You are learning how
In the helpless water
It is with our skill
We live in what kills us.

JOHN N. MORRIS

John N. Morris was educated at the Augusta Military Academy, Hamilton College, and Columbia University. At present he teaches eighteenth-century English literature at Washington University in St. Louis. He is the author of a critical study, VERSIONS OF THE SELF: STUDIES IN ENGLISH AUTOBIOGRAPHY (1966), *and of two earlier books of poems,* GREEN BUSINESS (1970) *and* THE LIFE BESIDE THIS ONE (1975).